DECORATIVE
Wreaths
AND
Garlands

4579 Decorative Wreaths and Garlands
Published in 1999 by CLB, an imprint of
Quadrillion Publishing Ltd of
Godalming Business Centre, Woolsack Way,
Godalming, Surrey, GU7 1XW, England

Distributed in the USA by
Quadrillion Publishing Inc.,
230 Fifth Avenue, New York 10001

ISBN 1-84100-032-9
Printed in Hong Kong

PHOTOGRAPHY: Nelson Hargreaves

DESIGN: Philip Clucas, MSIAD

EDITOR: Joseph F Ryan, PhD

DECORATIVE
Wreaths
AND
Garlands

Pamela Westland

CLB

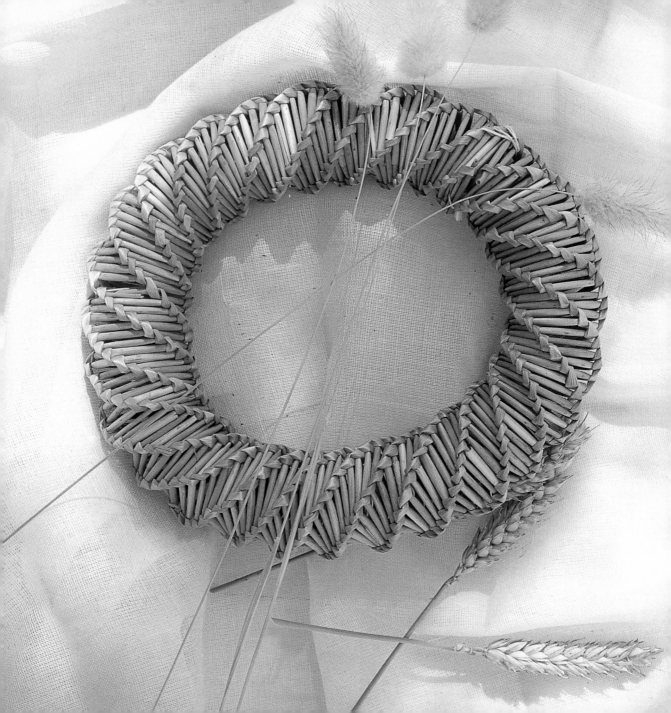

CONTENTS

Introduction *pages 6 – 13*

Making Wreaths and Garlands *pages 14 – 19*

Preparing Decorative Materials *pages 20 – 25*

Spring *pages 26 – 55*

High Summer *pages 56 – 81*

Late Summer *pages 82 – 113*

Winter *pages 114 – 143*

Acknowledgments *page 144*

INTRODUCTION

A hoop of honey-gold catkins and mimosa created as a wall decoration, just because it's spring; a garland of gossamer net and scented flowers ringed around a table arranged for a high summer wedding in a country garden; a table ring of glowing vegetables and bright berries destined to shine from harvest through to Thanksgiving; a hoop of evergreen leaves and gilded cherubim to hang on the door as a welcome sign—these and the many other wreaths and garlands designed for this book share a common ancestry, the decorations created in celebration of the seasonal festivals in ancient times. In those days, concurrently in diverse cultures throughout the world, people created wreaths which, because of their completeness of form, a continuous circle, came to represent continuity, security, fertility—a successful crop harvest year on year—eternal love, and even life itself.

Down the ages and with the application of lateral thinking, wreaths have been vested with more homey symbolism, most recently that of welcome, friendship, and hospitality. The evergreen wreaths we hang on our doors and walls at Thanksgiving and Christmas time are direct descendants of the ones hung around the necks of those who were victorious on the battleground or the sports arena, and the boughs of light-reflecting leaves brought in to lighten the dark days of winter.

Garlands, too, were created as meaningful expressions of hope and joy, thankfulness and obeisance. What evil spirit would have dared to enter a

Right: A garland of gossamer net, trailing willow leaves and dreamy, romantic flowers, creates the perfect ambience for a country midsummer wedding.

portal festooned with ribbons of foliage and flowers; what festival scene have been complete if the trees and tables, pedestals and pillars were not draped and encircled with floral garlands? The decorations we create today, floral ribbons winding around balcony rails and church pillars, and draped across table fronts and mantelpieces, justify the ancient belief in at least one element of symbolism, that of continuity.

TOOLS AND EQUIPMENT

While the joy derived from these decorations remains unchanged, the techniques available to us have altered considerably. A small collection of the "tools of the trade" makes it possible to extend the scope and range of the designs, and compose them more easily and quickly.

The introduction of absorbent floral foam rings and blocks represents a near-revolution in the art, making it possible to provide fresh plant material with a constant moisture source that many people find more reliable and less messy than damp moss. There is still a place for this natural material which, once thoroughly dampened, can be enclosed in a sausage-shaped roll of wire mesh netting, and formed into wreaths and garlands of any size and scale.

Creating the foundation or core of wreaths and garlands can be a therapeutic and aesthetically pleasing part of their composition, reminiscent of the days when young children made daisy chains and farm workers plaited straw and twisted it into rings and other shapes. Times have changed, and we are spoilt for choice among the ready-made ring bases available in florists and specialty stores. Many styles are almost an art form in themselves and, if the ring form is to be glimpsed at all, should be chosen with the color and style of the finished design in mind. Choose from types as varied as smooth white willow, gnarled and knobbly clematis or vine stems, plaited straw, cut dried grass, twisted paper coil, and many others. None of these types offers plant material a moisture source, but this can be provided in one of two ways: by binding on blocks of soaked floral foam, wrapped in plastic wrap to prevent seepage, or by inserting the stems of fresh flowers or foliage in orchid phials filled with water. Neither of these ploys makes attractive viewing, and the decoration must be designed so that the source of moisture remains a well-hidden secret.

FIXING MATERIALS

Techniques described for the projects shown throughout the book demonstrate the effectiveness of a few items of special equipment and purpose-made materials. Aesthetics apart, it is easier, for example, to bind a succession of fresh-flower posies to a twig ring base with green garden twine than with dried grass stems or stripped willow.

Colorless twine, green twine, fine string, raffia, and silver floral wire and green floral wire (both of which are sold on rolls) can all be used to bind plant materials to the base, and to bind clusters of stems into posies or bunches. In many cases, these binding materials are interchangeable; the choice of one in favor of another may depend on availability, or the prospect of any show-through factor. Silver roll wire, though widely used, can be most obtrusive if even the shortest length of it becomes visible in a finished decoration.

Floral wires, also known as stub wires, have a range of uses. They are sold in packets in a variety of lengths and thicknesses, of which medium is the most versatile, and can be used as false stems for dried flowers, cones, and other seedheads. Cut into short lengths and bent into U-shaped staples, they can take the place of special floral pins to fix posies and other materials to a twig base, or to secure handfuls of moss or hay to a foam ring or sphere.

Adhesives are increasingly used in floral art, offering a quicker and often less obtrusive means of attaching decorative materials to the core. All-purpose glue and hot glue are alternative options, always with the caution that hot glue can cause severe burns, and must be used with extreme care. Flowers which have been dried in desiccants and have little or no stem, sprays of dried leaves, dried apple or orange rings, small dried vegetables, blown eggshells, Christmas trinkets, and fresh flower stems and posies can all become attached to wreath and garland forms quickly and easily, with just a dab of glue.

THE CUTTING EDGE

There should be a plant health warning attached to blunt or inappropriate cutting tools. To avoid damaging the plant and shortening the shelf life of cut stems, it is important to use good quality, sharp cutting tools. Pruning shears are best suited for use with woody stemmed plants, such as holly and shrub roses; florist's scissors may be used for less resistant flower and foliage stems, and also to cut twine and silver floral wire, but only wire cutters are suitable for use with more substantial wires, and especially stub wires and wire netting. Household scissors have their uses, to cut raffia and ribbons, string and twine. A craft knife is useful for stripping off unwanted leaves, and a kitchen knife is essential to cut blocks of absorbent and dry floral foam.

A GOOD SOAKING

Whenever fresh plant materials are to be arranged in wreaths and garlands, and especially when the design precludes a source of moisture, the cut stems need to be immersed in cool water in a cool place, away from

Left: Cottage garden flowers combine wonderfully well with fresh herbs to make a garland of heady scent and dazzling color.

strong sunlight. So a collection of deep containers, such as buckets and bowls, is useful. Once the plants have been arranged, they need frequent showers of cool water from a fine mist spray and so this, too, should be part of your accessory kit. Remember to remove table decorations from vulnerable surfaces to avoid damage, returning them to the display site only when the external moisture has evaporated and there is no further risk of spoilage.

FRILLS AND FURBELOWS

An ivy-covered ring surrounding a posy of spring flowers and furbished with a gossamer ribbon bow; a scrumptious cake topped with a garland of marzipan fruits and encircled with a band of filmy ribbon; a wreath frame tightly wrapped around with overlapping bands of rich velvet; and a Shaker-style ring of dried apple slices topped by a twist of cotton gingham—gossamer-fine or staunchly practical, ribbons so often provide the finishing touch to wreath and garland designs. Color coordinated and chosen for their contrasting textures, twists and twirls of ribbon can complement compositions of natural materials and folk-art fantasies. Be sure that the ribbons are trim and well-pressed. And if you are tying, for example, a multi-loop bow for the first time, practice it first with tape or cord.

From spring through high summer, and late summer to winter, we hope that the designs throughout this book will prove that decorative wreaths and garlands not only have centuries of tradition behind them, but a long, bright future ahead.

Right: A gossamer ribbon makes a splendid "finishing touch" to a posy of freshly-cut flowers.

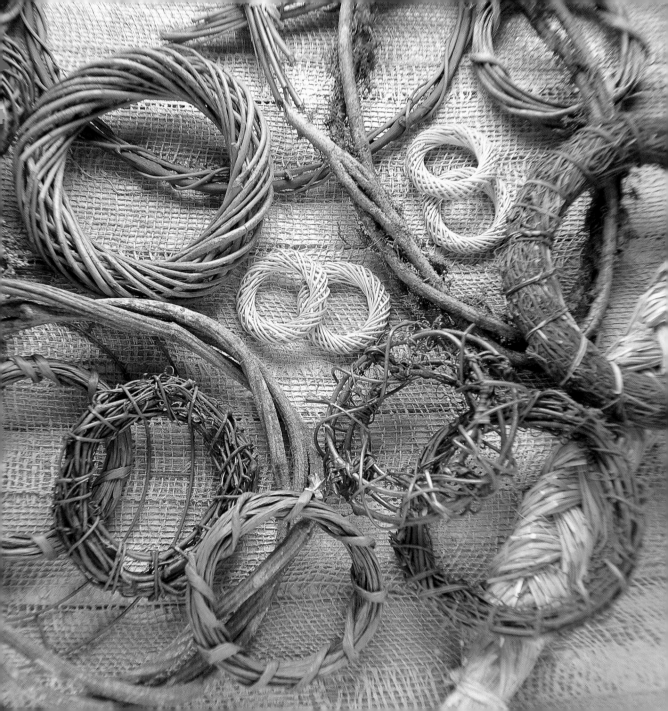

MAKING WREATHS AND GARLANDS

The design of wreaths and garlands has evolved from the early beginnings, when the decorations were created either without any natural core material at all, or on hoops and ropes made from twisted, supple stems with self-binding. Even now, when so many types of wreath base are readily available in florists and other specialty stores, it can be rewarding to make your own from soft stems such as grass and wild carrot, or from woody but supple stems of weeping willow, clematis, and vine.

When natural stems are used, they need be only partially covered with flowers, foliage, and other decorative materials, so that exposed areas can form an intrinsic part of the design. When heavy-duty rope, for example, is used as the core material for a garland, or when a decoration is created on a wreath base of preformed dry or absorbent stem-holding foam, then a complete coverup is essential. This can be achieved by the placement of edge-to-edge flowers and foliage, positioned so that there is no show-through, or by first covering the core or base with a sympathetic natural material such as dry hay or sphagnum moss.

STEP 1

To make a wreath base or a continuous garland core, bind together a cluster of supple stems, in this case weeping willow stripped of its leaves. If the stems are not supple enough to form into a circle, soak them in water for an hour or more, then drain them. Gather the stems into bunches of eight to ten and then, if part of the base is to be left uncovered, bind them with another similar stem. This is called "whipping." If none of the base will show, it is easier to bind it with green garden twine. To form the core into a wreath base, overlap the ends and bind them securely.

STEP 2

Double-wire ring frames, which are available from florists both in flat and slightly "dished" forms, can be covered with dry hay or sphagnum moss as a natural base for decoration with dried flowers and seedheads, nuts and cones, and fruit and vegetables. Attach a length of twine or roll wire to the ring, take a handful of the covering material, and bind it round and round so that the binding is concealed within its depth. Fasten off the binding when the ring is covered.

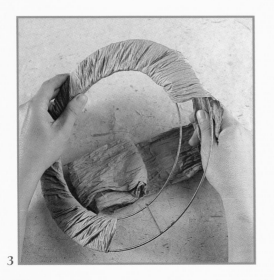

STEP 3

A flat double ring frame can be bound with unfurled paper ribbon, or with other decorative ribbons, as a base for a dried flower wreath.

Wrap one end of the ribbon over the ring. Paper ribbon will stay in place without fixing; other types might need securing with glue. Bind the ribbon round the ring, overlapping it all the way round. Fasten off the end and glue it, if necessary.

Attach a matching bow, and decorate the ring by gluing on individual dried flowers or small posies.

STEP 4

Floral foam rings can be made visually acceptable by covering them with dry hay or moss, an act of concealment suitable when the ring is to be decorated with woody stems or rigid, dried stems. Slender or supple stalks can be difficult to locate through the mesh of fibers. Take small handfuls of the hay or moss, and locate them around the top and sides of the ring with floral wire bent into U-shaped staples, or with floral pins.

5

6

STEP 5

Wreath forms made of twisted vine twigs can
be completely or partly covered with fresh or
dried flowers attached either individually or
in bunches. Place the flower stems against the
wreath base at whatever angle the design
dictates, and locate the stems by pressing a
floral pin or a U-shaped bent wire staple over
them and into the mesh of twigs. Bend back
the wire ends on the reverse of the wreath, to
avoid pricks and scratches. Position each posy
so that the flower heads conceal the stems
of the one before.

STEP 6

Flowers which have been dried with
desiccants and have little or no stalk can be
glued to a wreath base or garland core
without the need to attach false stems. Run a
little hot glue or all-purpose glue over the
base of the flower, or along one side of a
spray, and press it in place. If using hot
glue, take great care not to get
any onto your fingers.

7

8

STEP 7

When you are using thick twine, rope or cord as the core material for a garland, you can give it more substance and a more natural look by covering it with dry hay or sphagnum moss. To do this, tie twine to one end of the rope, wrap small handfuls of the covering material around it, and bind them on with the twine. Fasten off the twine securely at the other end of the rope. Shake the garland gently before adding the wired nuts, cones, foliage or flowers, so that it sheds any loose fibers.

STEP 8

Garland cores covered with hay or moss provide a natural-looking base for foliage decorations at Thanksgiving and Christmas time. To cover the core with, for example, evergreens and berries, compose them into mixed bunches and bind them onto the rope with green garden twine or green floral wire.

To compose a garland that will be draped over a fireplace or an arch, measure and mark the center. Start at one end, binding on the first bunch or spray with the stems facing inwards. Bind on the next spray so that the foliage tips cover the stem ends, and so on to the center. Work from the other end to the center in the same way and bind on a decorative feature such as a ribbon bow to conceal the stems at the center.

PREPARING
DECORATIVE MATERIALS

O nce you know how to wire flowers, cones, nuts, shells, and other decorative materials quickly and easily, you will be able to incorporate them into a wide range of wreath and garland designs. Flowers that have been dried in desiccants, and others such as strawflowers which readily become detached from their natural stems, can be mounted on floral wires, which are then bound with floral tape in a neutral color, and used in the same way as fresh flowers.

Fresh and dried flowers can be gathered into mixed and colorful posies before being bound or glued to wreath bases and garland cores, and bunches of twigs can be wired together and added to countrified wreath designs to give them a casual look.

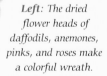

Left: The dried flower heads of daffodils, anemones, pinks, and roses make a colorful wreath.

STEP 1

To compose a wreath or garland design with a random mixture of fresh flower types and colors, you can gather the materials first into small bunches. Select flowers that complement each other well in terms of size and shape (one extra large flower in a bunch would tend to obscure the others), and bind the stems with raffia or silver roll wire. Cut the stems level, and keep the flowers in water until you are ready to make up the decoration. Once the flowers are in place, and no longer have a moisture source, spray them with a fine mist of cool water. If possible, position the decoration where it will be away from direct heat or strong sunlight.

STEP 2

Make up posies of dried flowers, grasses, and seedheads in a similar way. Since many dried plant materials are brittle and easily damaged, take care not to crowd or crush them. Protect the most delicate flowers, such as daffodils or rosebuds, by surrounding them with other less vulnerable materials such as hare's tail grasses and strawflowers. Bind the stems with silver roll wire, fine twine or raffia.

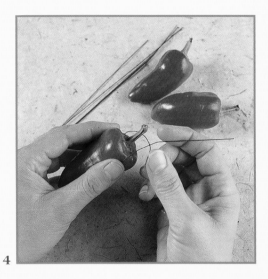

STEP 3

To create a false stem on fir and larch cones, insert a medium-gauge floral wire below the two lowest layers of "petals." Bring the two ends of the wire together beneath the cone, cross them over and twist them together. The wires can then be inserted in twig wreath bases or twisted around garland cores.

STEP 4

Small, firm vegetables (such as eggplants, zucchini, sweet corn, and chilies) make decorative and contrasting additions to country-style or harvest wreaths and garlands. If you wish to eat the vegetables after they have served a decorative purpose, it is best to spear them on wooden toothpicks or satay sticks, and not to pierce them with wires which might corrode.

To mount the vegetables on wires, push through a medium- or heavy-gauge floral wire close to the base. Bring the ends together underneath and twist them to form a thick "stem."

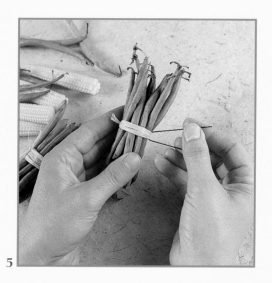

STEP 5

Sometimes it is more appropriate to tie natural elements such as small young vegetables into bunches, and then attach them to the wreath base or garland core by threading a floral wire through the binding. Raffia makes a sympathetic binding for bunches of young green beans, carrots, miniature sweet corn and mange tout peas. Use a rubber band to keep the bunch of vegetables together initially, then tie them with several strands of raffia. Finish with a knot or bow and slip off the rubber band.

STEP 6

Gluing nuts such as walnuts, pecans, almonds, and chestnuts into clusters and then threading a floral wire through the gaps is quicker and easier than wrapping each one with a wire. Use hot glue or all-purpose glue to make up the clusters, taking care not to let any hot glue burn your fingers.

STEP 7

However carefully you handle them, the daisy-like strawflowers easily snap from their natural stems. So when you want to include them in a posy, or attach them to a garland when gluing is not appropriate—for example, if the core is covered with hay—you might need to insert a false stem. Push a medium-gauge floral wire from the back up through the center of the flower. Bend a small hook in the top of the wire and gently pull it downwards, so that the hook is concealed in the flower center.

STEP 8

Whenever you have mounted natural materials onto false wire stems, and the wires might show in the finished decoration, bind them with floral tape (gutta percha). This narrow tape, which is available in a range of colors including brown, cream, and green, is self-adhesive and sticks to itself as you overlap each binding.

Wrap the tape tightly round the wire just below the flower head then, holding the wire in one hand and pulling the tape taut with the other, twist the wire so that the tape wraps evenly round it. Twist the tape tightly at the end and cut it off.

Spring

Since ancient times, spring has been celebrated as the season of renewal and rebirth. Buds bursting on trees and hedges along the waysides, flowers burgeoning in the gardens, and suddenly the world is a brighter and more colorful place. Rejoice in this new-found wealth of natural materials, and use them to create wreaths and garlands that capture the joyful mood.

FESTIVAL FLOWERS

Above: Arrange the hellebores and heather until the surface of the foam ring is almost hidden, then add the feature flowers.

Right: Cascades of pale green hellebores take the place of foliage in a sun-bright table ring of the season's brightest flowers.

Celebrate a bright, sunny day; the coming of spring; the Easter festival; or a special family occasion. Highlight a party table with one of these spectacular floral wreaths, one an outer ring of ivy leaves overlapping to form a patchwork of glossy greens encircling a bowl of vivid spring blooms, the other a circle of sun-bright flowers decorated with tapers in toning colors. Here daffodils and irises, hellebores and heathers, come together in an exuberant floral ring that would look pretty anywhere, any time.

Place either of the wreaths center-stage on a buffet table for a springtime party under the sun or the stars. Dress it up for a teatime celebration by placing it on your prettiest lace cloth and complementing it with your finest china, or put the ring on a pedestal by giving it pride of place on a side table or wine table.

The floral wreath is composed of short-stemmed flower sprays and individual blooms arranged in a wet floral foam ring. Clusters of ice-green Corsican hellebores provide the ground cover, the stems angled this way and that so that the flowers tumble down over inner and outer rims, almost totally concealing the foam. Sprays of pinky mauve heather are directed horizontally around the ring, setting the scene for a blaze of daffodils and irises.

Slender tapers in matching colors are arranged in fanburst formation at opposite sides of the ring. Keep a spare packet of party tapers on hand once you light them—their pretty pinpoints of light are somewhat short-lived, and could be down to the level of the flowers almost before you have time to notice.

THE IVY RING

As it is springtime, forget all the preconceived notions you have had about evergreen wreaths—welcome rings speckled with winter holly berries hanging on frost-sparkled doors. This one is different. Glossy green ivy leaves covering a dry floral foam ring create a perfect frame for a cluster of deep mauve and brilliant yellow flowers.

To cover the ring, select flat, medium-sized leaves which are heavily veined; they look more decorative that way. If the leaves are too small, the task will take longer, and if they are too large, they will not wrap neatly around the ring.

Use all-purpose glue or hot glue to stick the leaves in place, starting at the base of the ring and tucking the edge of the first layer under for a neat finish. Work in rows, around the outer rim, across the top and down the inner rim, tucking under the final row to neaten the edge. A bowl of water in the center of the ring will keep generations of flowers fresh. You can change them (and the water) every few days. A trailing gossamer ribbon bow adds a delicate finishing touch.

Left: A central posy of purple and golden flowers is dramatically framed by a glistening ring of overlapping ivy leaves.

HEARTS & FLOWERS

S t. Valentine's Day has a long tradition of secret or enigmatic messages, of exchanged tokens and renewed avowals of love. Celebrate the occasion with a romantic dinner *à deux*, and create a delicate confection garlanded with sugar-sweet berries, flowers, and rose petals.

While no era has had a monopoly on romance, it was the Victorians who elevated the expression of love to an art form, and made St. Valentine's Day a red-letter day in any young lover's calendar.

Greetings cards exchanged to mark the occasion bore meaningful images of red roses and forget-me-nots, and equally flowery verses or messages. One addressed to "my pretty bird" asks the direct question, "Will you come and dwell with me among the flowers?" Another, depicting nosegays under a toadstool umbrella, declares, "My heart is where true love reposes; I'll strew for you a bed of roses."

Our possibly more pragmatic interpretation of "a bed of roses" takes the form of two confections decorated with sugar-frosted roses and petals, pineapple mint, a symbol in Victorian times of worth and merit, heartsease and pansies, for thoughts, and strings of redcurrants, signifying fruitfulness.

The dessert, put on a glass pedestal stand for the occasion, is a fruit mousse made by setting strawberry purée and strawberry yogurt with dissolved gelatin. Turned out of a ring mold, the dessert itself takes the form of a

Right: A strawberry dessert set in a ring mold is
garlanded with sugared fruit and rose petals.

Above: Sugar-frosted and dried in an airing cupboard, the fruit and flowers are ready to be arranged.

Above: Lightly beaten egg white and superfine sugar are all you need to add sparkle to fruit, flowers, and scented leaves.

garland, and is ringed around with strings of sugared redcurrants overlapped to make a continuous circle. Arrange these and the frosted leaves and flowers just before serving, to prevent any moisture from softening and spoiling the decoration.

The heart-shaped sponge cake, covered with rolled fondant frosting, is decorated with a nosegay of sugar-crusted herbs and flowers. In Victorian times, such symbolic embellishments would have been treasured under a glass dome as a precious keepsake.

To Frost the Flowers

Check that any flowers and leaves you use are edible. The list that follows will ensure that your decoration is not only pretty but meaningful.

Select from plants that have not been sprayed with harmful insecticides. Wash and thoroughly dry them, if necessary.

Lightly beat an egg white in a small bowl and brush it lightly over each petal and leaf. Hold the plant material with tweezers and allow any excess liquid to drain. Too much egg white will mask the plants' pretty characteristics.

Spread the sugared items on a wire rack or silicone paper and leave them to dry for several hours in a warm, dry place such as an airing cupboard. Store them between sheets of kitchen paper in an airtight container.

Above: A heart-shaped cake spells romance even before it is decorated with flowers that symbolize true love and thoughtfulness.

Edible flowers and their romantic associations

APPLE BLOSSOM..........*temptation*

BROOM....................*humility*

CARNATION, PINK.......*a woman's love*

CARNATION, RED........*my heart is affected*

CLOVER...................*be mine!*

DAISY.....................*I share your sentiments*

FORGET–ME–NOT.......*true love*

HONEYSUCKLE...........*bond of love*

JASMINE..................*sensuality*

LILAC, PURPLE..........*first emotion of love*

MINT.....................*virtuous love*

PANSY....................*think of me*

ROSE, RED................*true love*

ROSEBUD.................*young love*

VIOLET, BLUE............*faithfulness in love*

VIOLET, WHITE..........*innocence*

EXTENDED PLEASURES

The flowers that bloom in the spring have the potential for so much more than transient beauty. Buy them by the armful when they crowd the markets, or cut them from the garden if you can bear to, and dry them batch by batch. Then, with a selection of paper-crisp flowers from dazzling yellow to deepest purple, you can create long-lasting garlands and wreaths that will shine on the dullest days. And no amount of bulk buying will seem an extravagance.

You can capture all the glory of spring's loveliest flowers for as long as they give you pleasure—until the first golden daffodils and paintbox-colored tulips bloom again, and the air is once more heady with the scent of mimosa. These are among the most successful of flowers to dry, most of them by means of a desiccant, when they lose none of their shape or form, color or glamour in the process.

Once they are dried, you can use the short-stemmed flowers just the way they are. Glue them around a twig wreath to create a pretty table center or wall decoration, or compose them, tulips and daffodils, anemones and irises, among dried herb leaves on a bundle of twigs.

With a little more time, you can mount each dried flower and short-stemmed spray of mimosa onto floral wires, bind the false stems with floral tape, and consider the flowers just-like-fresh.

Right: Ring a ring of posies, each one wrapped in cellophane paper and arranged around the sides of a deep, decorative dish.

Above: Sprinkle flowers with desiccant so that it covers every part of each surface.

Above: Hanging flowers upside down on a rack helps to keep them in perfect shape.

A pretty nosegay of dried flowers tied with raffia and placed on each plate around the dinner table is a delightful take-home memento for guests. Compose more and more bunches, wrap each one in seethrough paper for protection and added sheen, and you can arrange them garland-style around a deep, decorative dish.

DRYING FLOWERS

Gather flowers for drying on a dry day, once the dew has evaporated, and select only perfect ones. Cut the stems about 1 inch below the base of each flower. To dry them in silica gel crystals, the most efficient desiccant, you can use a microwave on low power, a conventional oven on the lowest setting, or use an airtight container at room temperature.

Sprinkle a layer of crystals in a suitable container (microwave safe, ovenproof or airtight) and place the flowers well apart. Spoon the desiccant around them, supporting extended petals and filling every cavity, then cover the flowers with a ½-inch layer of desiccant.

Place an open container in a microwave for five to seven minutes, depending on the capacity of the appliance and the volume of the plant material, or in a conventional oven for about 30 minutes. At room temperature, in a covered container, the flowers might take two or three days to dry thoroughly. Check at intervals and remove the flowers from the desiccant as soon as they are dry and the crystals have cooled.

Above: Desiccant–dried flowers mounted on wires and sprays of mimosa dried by
hanging in a warm, airy room are made up into posies, one for each guest.

Leave the flowers for a few hours before arranging them. You can either
spread them on a wire cooling rack, or bind the short stems with silver roll
wire and hang them upside down. This method has the advantage of providing
the binding material you need if you are going to mount the flowers on floral
wires to create false stems. Before arranging them, brush the flowers with a
small craft brush to remove the powdery deposit of the desiccant.

HEDGEROW COLOR

Above: The essence of the countryside in spring is represented in an asymmetrical wreath combining catkins and mimosa bound onto a twisted twig ring.

Left: For greater impact, display the catkin ring as part of a still-life group, with a jug of tall hazel twigs and a basket of daffodils.

Harness the pollen-rich gold of catkin tassles or the sugar-almond pinks of Prunus blossom to create two of the season's most unusual wreaths. Spring flowers in brighter, deeper shades reinforce the subtle hedgerow colors in both a wayward wall decoration and a compact candle ring.

Clusters of catkins hanging from birch or hazel, alder or willow represent the essence of springtime along the waysides and hedgerows, and have an appealing design potential. Cut a few twigs (or buy a bunch at the market) and arrange them with seasonal flowers in a casual way, creating an informal wreath to decorate your home or a country church at Eastertime.

In the wall decoration, the angular shoots are bound onto a slender, twisted twig ring in a way that is reminiscent of sparks flying from a rotating catherine wheel. The more unruly the stems appear to be, and the more diverse the angles, the more natural looking and intriguing the wreath will be.

With the catkins held firmly in place with green roll wire, the inner circle of the decoration is color enriched with thick sprays of fluffy mimosa flowers and frondy leaves, bound onto the

Below: Select a floral foam ring with a diameter of about 4 inches greater than that of the willow ring, so that you have ample room to position the surrounding stems.

Right: The woven willow ring performs a decorative rather than a functional role in this unusual table ring in which Prunus blossom and mimosa combine with border pinks and nerines.

wreath base and, at the same time, concealing the bare ends of the twigs.

Hung in a dry, airy place, the catkins and mimosa will dry naturally and almost imperceptibly, and the decoration will be a delightful reminder that, outside, it is already spring.

THE CANDLE RING

The wreath-within-a-wreath construction of the candle ring celebrates two perfect unions, between willow and false cherry blossom, and between hedgerow beauty and romantically pretty garden flowers.

The woven willow ring, varnished to put it even more in the spotlight, is wired to a wet floral foam ring with U-shaped staples. This simple piece of construction work completed, branches of Prunus blossom are snipped short, any bare twigs discarded, and arranged evenly around the foam. Short sprays of mimosa follow the same outline, before nerines and border pinks are arranged randomly at varying angles. A stubby pink candle in the center casts a warm glow over a decoration that has romantic overtones.

LOOKS DELICIOUS!

Pretty as a picture, a hoop of orchids and pinks outlines a tempting presentation of small party cakes, sugar-frosted in pastel pinks and greens. And then, ringing the changes, the "iced fancies" become the garland, arranged around a Victorian-style posy of sweetly-scented flowers.

When it comes to arranging a party table, for a baptism or a young child's birthday perhaps, the concept of a garland is open to wide interpretation. You can compose the flowers to run rings around the food, outlining a dessert, a celebration cake or a plate of small confections with a circlet of individual blooms, or highlight a presentation of savories with a ring of intertwined herb stems such as rosemary and golden thyme speckled with a scattering of marigold petals or deep blue cornflowers. As the flowers and foliage will be without a moisture source, be sure to give them a good, long drink of water in a cool place before arranging them.

Although there will always be the implied direction to "Don't eat the daisies," whenever the plant material is likely to come into contact with the food, it is advisable to choose flowers which are both decorative and edible. Fortunately, the choice is very wide. When young children are among the guests, and a free-style decoration is vulnerable, it is a good idea to thread or bind the flowers onto a length of flexible wire.

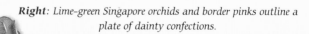

Right: Lime-green Singapore orchids and border pinks outline a plate of dainty confections.

Left: Short sprays of baby's-breath (gypsophila) contrast delightfully with the many-petalled roses and pinks that make up the central posy.

THE CAKE RING

Toning flowers, which include border pinks and cream roses, pale green hellebores and baby's-breath (*gypsophila*), are composed into a compact posy, their stems tied with narrow ribbon and held in a deep glass bowl surrounded by concentric rings of mouthwatering cakes. It is true that the first guests might feel diffident about breaking the symmetry or spoiling the presentation, but not for long.

TASTES DELICIOUS!

A few edible flowers and leaves that would be suitable to ring around a presentation of sweet or savory foods have already been listed. Others you might like to consider include borage, border pink, elderflower, freesia, geranium, lavender, lily, marjoram, mimosa, mint, nasturtium, orchid, primrose, sweet william, and viola.

NESTING INSTINCTS

A colorful nest shape constructed on a wire frame plays host to a clutch of hens' eggs dyed in primary colors and other strong shades. The theme is echoed in the companion Eastertime decoration, in which a clutch of eggs is encircled by a ring of planted primroses.

Plain-dyed eggs and springtime flowers make a fabulous Eastertime partnership, each element rivaling the other for compulsive viewing. At each place around the breakfast table you could set a colored egg on moss in a miniature flowerpot and surround it with a "daisy-chain" garland of primroses or pansies. Or, reversing the roles, you could arrange, say, tulips and mimosa in a bowl in the center of a flat dish or tray and surround the flowers with eggs in a neat circle.

Our Easter table decorations are extended versions of these ideas. To get the festival off to a bright start, there is a plant grouping that could scarcely be more vibrant. Pots of primroses from buttery yellow to deep purple stand edge to edge around a basketwork tray. Remember to put a layer of broken "crocks," pebbles or gravel in the base of each pot, to avoid waterlogging, and stand each one on a waterproof saucer to resist seepage. The pot in the center is filled with dry moss and lichen, and piled high with eggs dyed in toning colors.

Right: *A planted garland of potted primroses arranged around a clutch of dyed eggs would brighten any kitchen or breakfast table.*

TO MAKE THE NEST

Emulate the care birds take to construct their nests at this time of year, and make a decorative look-alike with moss, dried flower sprays, and a few found feathers.

The base of the nest is a square of wire mesh netting about 24 inches across. This is folded four times, bringing each corner into the center and then (protecting your hands with gloves) scrunched up and folded over at the sides to make the circular walls.

Below: *The ingredients that make up the decorative nest on the opposite page—a framework of wire mesh, dried mimosa and statice, moss, and feathers.*

Above: *Dyed eggs take on a speckled appearance that emphasizes their natural textures.*

With the framework made, it is then a matter of foraging for lining materials. Handfuls of dried hay and moss, and sprays of dried statice and mimosa, are pushed and threaded in among the mesh of wires until the shape is covered all round. A few extra flower sprays are tucked in where more color is needed, and a handful of pheasants' feathers added last of all. The colored eggs might be held back until the morning, as a breakfast-time surprise for the children.

To Dye the Eggs

If you are planning to eat the eggs, dye them with edible food coloring. If not, you can use egg dye or fabric dye, both available from craft stores.

1 Hardboil the eggs for 10 minutes in the usual way, then drain them.

2 Mix enough of your chosen dye with 1 pint of hot water to achieve the depth of color you want. Stir in 2 tablespoons of vinegar and 1 tablespoon of salt, and leave to cool.

3 Add the eggs to the dye and leave them until they are the shade you like. Drain them on kitchen paper. Store any leftover dye in a covered jar for future use.

4 Once the eggs are dry, polish them if you wish with a few drops of olive oil on a soft, dry cloth.

SNOWFLAKE GARLANDS

Above: A continuous garland chain of linked plastic foam holders simplifies the construction of an articulated inner core.

Right: The soft framework of Queen Anne's lace contrasts daintily with pastel-colored marguerites, and with the cornflower posy on top of the celebration cake.

Queen Anne's lace or sheep's parsley, sweet cicely or elderflower, gather them as and where you may, these creamy-white umbellifer plants brought in from the wild inspire the prettiest of spring garlands. Supplement one of these floral ribbons with more compact flowers in white or parchment tints, or highlight the lacy flowers at intervals with more vibrant and colorful blooms. Either way, these "snowflake" garlands capture the essence of the countryside in spring.

Hang a wayside garland in a window where, against the light, it will seem ephemeral and look especially pretty. Drape it around a table where, framing a celebration cake or a selection of tempting party fare, it will complement rather then detract from the food. Or compose a short section of the decoration, or a matching pair, and hang them vertically to accent a doorway, an arch or porch.

The core of the garland, the hidden support for a decoration of this kind, can be as simple as a length of thick rope, which is pliable enough to hang in soft falls and drapes, in the kind of curves that look good across the front of a tablecloth. But, offering the plant materials no moisture source, a rope core is a short-term option. For a longer-lasting decoration, you can use blocks of wet floral foam in one of several ways.

Above: *Draped beneath a window, a garland composed mainly of plants gathered in the wild forms a delightful link with the countryside.*

If flexibility and natural-looking drapes are not important to the design, you can wrap blocks of damp foam first in plastic wrap and then in a roll of wire mesh netting, to enclose them in a long sausage shape. Another way is to bind the blocks of wrapped foam to a length of rope, which will provide the flexibility, or thread each block onto a floral wire and hook the ends of the neighboring wires together to form a continuous, articulated chain.

A ready-made and more user-friendly version of the interlinked principle makes short work of the process. The damp foam (wrapped in plastic wrap to avoid seepage) is held in plastic cages which are hooked on one to another until the garland reaches the required length.

Whatever holding material you use, begin by arranging a groundwork of closely-packed flowers and foliage to conceal it. The slightest glimpse of sturdy rope or glistening foam detracts from the romance of the decoration. Add feature flowers if you wish at random intervals, the heads facing this way and that for a natural and informal look. Spray the completed garland with water and keep it in a cool place until just before the event.

When you hang it in position, have a few spare sprays of foliage and flowers ready—which means that they should have been cut several hours before, and given a good long drink of water. Then, if the garland twists and turns as you fix it, you will be able to fill in any gaps on the spot.

Left: Setting the scene for a wedding party, this vertical swag is composed of two of the plastic wire cages linked together with a twisted pearl bead necklace. The sweet cicely flowers contrast with lemon-yellow freesias, spray carnations, and spray chrysanthemums.

HIGH SUMMER

*A*s the temperature rises, colors seem
more fiery by the minute, and all around it is
impromptu party time, so relax some of the
guidelines, think laterally and bring some
unexpected elements, from shells to
strawberries, cakes to clothespins, into
your decorative orbit. It all adds
up to high summer high style.

HERBAL HARVEST

Pansies and marigolds, cornflowers and roses, pineapple mint and lady's mantle—it is hard to imagine a profusion of plant materials that, together, are more romantic, colorful, and aromatic. Harvest them in high summer to create stylish decorations that have their roots in traditional cottage gardens and backyards.

In country gardens where space was limited, and plants had to earn their keep in terms of culinary and medicinal usefulness, attention was not always paid to their size, shape or form. Herbs and other aromatic plants were often grown in tightly-packed clusters which gradually became intermingled, tumbled untidily together over border edges and brick paths, and presented a generally higgledy-piggledy picture.

In keeping with this charming yet practical tradition, it is appropriate to celebrate the glory of high summer by composing herbal decorations which echo this artless effect, emphasizing the brilliance of the colors first by grouping the flowers in all-of-a-kind posies, then by framing them in a network of blue and yellowy-green foliage.

Most herbs are readily available at garden centers, ready to be planted out in open ground or in containers. Many can be grown indoors on a sunny windowsill, where they will be both decorative and useful before you cut a sprig here and a spray there to form the basis of your decorations.

Right: A fresh and colorful wall wreath of herb flowers and leaves captures the essence of the cottage garden, perfectly set off against a rustic whitewashed door.

THE HERBAL WREATH

You can compose a wreath of fresh foliage and flowering herbs by binding them on to a vine wreath form. Cut all the plant materials well in advance, and put the stems deep in cool water in a cool place, preferably overnight. Cover the ring first with clusters of herbs such as santolina and lady's mantle, mint and marjoram, and add bunches of chives at intervals around the ring to branch off "catherine-wheel" style. Compose the bunches of four or five stems, according to their scale, and bind them onto the ring so that the heads of one posy conceal the stem ends of the previous one.

Spray the decoration with water and keep it in a cool place, even in the refrigerator, until the last moment. Especially on a hot or humid day, continue to spray the flowers at intervals, since this treatment will be the plants' sole moisture source.

Many of the herbs and flowers will dry *in situ*, thus greatly extending the life of the wreath. To achieve this long-term goal, select woody rather than fleshy herbs, evergreens and perennials in preference to annuals. Rosemary, bay, sage, and santolina foliage dry successfully in this way, as do sprays of lady's mantle leaves and flowers together. Among other flowering herbs, marjoram, chives, cornflowers, and rosebuds look prettiest for longest.

An alternative method, which makes it possible to include any flowers of your choice and still have a fresh-looking decoration several days later, is to compose the design on a wet floral foam ring. Cut the flower stems short and insert them in clusters for a massed effect; use a fine skewer to pierce a hole for slender or pliable stems. Chive leaves almost certainly will not "hold" in the foam at all. Wire them into bunches, twist the two ends of the wires together and insert those, and not the leaves, into the foam.

Above: *Pansies and pinks, pineapple mint and geranium flowers alternate with wisps of lady's mantle around the plate, and comprise the posy held in a "napkin ring" of tied chive leaves.*

WHEEL OF FRAGRANCE

To create a very different yet equally informal type of garland, compose a ring of herbs and flowers around each place at the table. Although the decoration looks entirely unpremeditated, ideally, it should not be. Stand all the stems in water before arranging them around the plates at the last moment.

SWEET INDULGENCES

Whether you are inviting neighbors to contribute to charity funds at a coffee morning, a few friends are coming in for a fashionable afternoon tea, or it's party time and you are offering a galaxy of irresistible gateaux, decorate the confections with garlands of fruit, foliage, and flowers and make them more tempting still.

A gateau can be as plain or fancy as you like, from a towering confection of "death by triple chocolate" to a rose-petal-scented sponge cake; a rich fruit cake covered with the smoothest of lemon frostings to a light-as-air angel food cake baked in a ring form pan. Whatever the recipe and whatever the occasion, look to a garland of edible decorations to add that final celebratory touch.

You might choose to edge a circular cake with a ring of soft fruits and attractive, variegated leaves. Scented geranium (pelargonium) leaves have just what it takes to frame a party-piece. If you are baking a plain cake of any type, you could place two or three of the leaves at the base of the pan for their flavor and fragrance to be absorbed.

Set a ring of the leaves around the serving dish to outline the cake, then another, of smaller leaves or sprays, to edge the top of it. Soft fruits like strawberries and raspberries contrast effectively with chocolate; blackberries and blueberries contrast less well, but evoke the height of sophistication. Choose firm, not-quite-ripe fruits that will not weep the juice onto the surface, and keep them separately in the refrigerator until the last minute, just before you need to arrange them.

Above: Melted chocolate blended with whipped cream makes a "fondue dip" for a circle of fresh fruit kebabs.

Right: Fondant icing leaf shapes in white and palest green are an alternative option to white chocolate ones to highlight a triple chocolate cake.

MAKE-BELIEVE FRUITS

Marzipan fruits have a longer display life than fresh ones, and tempt you to combine the produce of varied harvests. Apples and bananas, pears and peaches, most with a rosy glow, can be arranged garland-style with sprays of marzipan leaves or ones shaped from candied angelica. Think ahead when you are making or buying the decorations, and the matter of "portion control." Small fruits conveniently placed so that one will decorate each slice represent a fairer distribution of the goodies than too few large ones.

CHOCOLATE LEAVES

Leafy garlands have a festive air, whether they are wall-hung decorations or mouthwatering confections on top of cakes and desserts. Chocolate leaves are quick and easy to make. Use good quality bitter or white chocolate and melt it in a bowl over a pan of simmering, but not boiling, water.

Have everything else ready. You will need a few well-shaped rose leaves, washed and dried, a teaspoon and a wire cooling rack. Take the chocolate from the heat and, with the spoon, evenly coat one side of the leaf with it. A quick, stroking action gives the best results. Spread out the leaves, chocolate side up, to dry on the rack.

When the chocolate has set, carefully peel off and discard the rose leaves. Store the chocolate shapes between sheets of kitchen paper in an airtight tin.

GOING INTO FREE FALL

Above: No sunshade was ever more alluring! A stylish parasol is ringed around with blowsy roses and carnations. Now all you need is a hammock!

Right: Tied bunches of sweet william and cornflowers are kept in water until the time comes to arrange them.

I t's summer time, and the living is easy. Ignore the rules and hang the flower decorations. Hang them in bunches across a wreath form, from an iron coat rack on the wall, from the spokes of a garden umbrella, even the branches of a tree. Let the flowers go into free fall at the scene of a party, relax, and rejoice that it's summer.

Gathering flowers into bunches and posies, all of a kind or all mixed up, is one of the prettiest ways of displaying them. Carefree and casual, delightfully natural and charmingly understated, the nosegays can be formed into neat floral ribbons and compact garlands, as closely packed as any well-stocked flowerbed. Or they can be arranged to just go hang.

This is a concept that, by definition, should look unplanned, as if on the spur of the moment you had gathered up an armful of flowers and tied them up there and then. You can make the decorations that way, and for a truly impromptu occasion you might have to. But to keep the flowers fresh-looking for longest, once they are away from a moisture source and possibly in the full glare of the sun, collect them together overnight, or at least an hour or so ahead of the event.

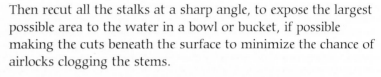

Left: Think vertically—tied bunches of sweet william pinned in opposite directions along a plaited straw base make an eye-catching wall decoration.

Above: A wreath of mixed flowers including lisianthus and pinks, cornflowers and antirrhinum bring a note of glamor to an iron garden chair.

Then recut all the stalks at a sharp angle, to expose the largest possible area to the water in a bowl or bucket, if possible making the cuts beneath the surface to minimize the chance of airlocks clogging the stems.

To save time at the last minute, arrange the flowers in bunches, creating color harmonies or vibrant clashes, as the mood takes you, and tie the stems with raffia. Leave them in water in a cool place until moments before the festivities begin.

HELD IN SUSPENSE

With the bunches tied up and ready, and all the other preparations in hand, it is just a matter of deciding how and where to hang them. Signal a welcome as guests approach by tying the flowers to the gate, adding two or three balloons for good measure. If there is a ceiling beam in the party area, tape or tack a line of upside-down bunches to form a vertical garland, like a floral pelmet or curtain, and tape more bunches around the top of an arch or doorway to form a half circle.

Tie elongated bunches to the back of dining chairs, and small posies around the rim of a serving table or a pedestal stand displaying a cake. Wire floral bunches or large, single blooms in varying directions around a twig ring or, for a vertical wall decoration, with the stems crisscrossing down the length of a thick raffia plait. Create floral garlands by hanging individual flowers from the spokes of garden umbrellas, but avoid using rose stems with thorns, and leave a suitable gap between the flowers for comfortable comings and goings.

STRAWBERRY FAIR

Clumps of moss and twisting, turning strawberry shoots make for outdoor-friendly decorations for porch or patio. Gather handfuls of green or gray moss to cover wreath forms and topiary shapes, then wind the strawberry runners around them, just the way they grow—haywire.

Dried moss and sweet-smelling hay are the perfect cover-up materials for less-than-beautiful wreath frames and garland cores. Bind them by the handful along the length of the rope at the heart of a garland and, if there is any show-through once it is decorated with flowers and foliage, it is only natural. Use these materials, too, to give substance to double-wire wreath frames, and to conceal floral foam rings completely before wiring on or inserting fruits or flowers.

In most cases, hay or moss used in this way becomes part of the "mechanics," the support material that will be hidden, or almost completely so, beneath sprays of foliage, clusters of nuts and cones, or a wealth of colorful flowers.

The decorations on these pages are different. The slender strawberry trails winding their way round and over the base material make no attempt to conceal it. Instead, the grass-green leaves and bright red fruits look all the more luscious and tempting for the contrast they create in form and textures.

Left: Whether it is displayed indoors or outside, this moss-covered wreath has a pastoral look that, especially in summer, is particularly appealing.

Right: Make this decoration when the strawberry bed needs thinning or tidying. Put all the shoots and any separate leaves in water until you need to use them.

Above: A wire ring frame, moss, green garden twine, U-shaped staples, and strawberry runners and fruit are the materials needed for the wreath shown on page 70.

THE STRAWBERRY TREE

It is immaterial what you choose for the ball shape of the topiary tree, since it will not be seen. You can use a sphere of intertwined twigs, like a hollow ball, which you can buy at some florists, or a floral foam ball which is more readily

Above: Take a twig wreath, entwine it with a few trails of rose leaves, wild roses or berries, and fill the center with luscious, wine-red cherries for a look that is the very essence of summer.

available. Push the ball firmly onto a stout stick and cover it with moss or hay, pinned on with floral pins or staples made from bent floral wire, then plant the stick in a flowerpot. One way to do this is to fix a heavy metal pinholder in the base of the pot, impale the stick on that and pack around it with floral clay. Another way is to line the pot with a thin sheet of plastic foam (to prevent cracking), insert the stick and partly fill the pot with plaster of Paris.

Leave room for a layer of potting compost, and plant a few small strawberry or wild strawberry plants to trail over the rim. Wind more and more shoots around the ball until the moss is about half covered. Just before visitors are expected, cheat and pin a few fresh fruits among the leaves.

ROUND IN CIRCLES

The strawberry-leaf wreath shown on page 70 captures the ambience of a well-ordered and fruitful kitchen garden, with tempting berries nestling among the leaves. Cover a wire ring frame or a twig ring with moss or hay, binding it tightly with green garden twine that will disappear into its depth.

Cut long strawberry runners, leave them in water for a long drink, then pin them onto the wreath base with floral pins or floral wires bent into U-shaped staples. Add fresh fruits or even false ones for effect.

CHILL FACTORS

W hen the temperature's rising, and ice-cold desserts and drinks are called for, play it cool with flower decorations, too. Create a garland of summer's prettiest blooms to outline a chilled dessert bowl, and preserve a ring of edible flowers and scented leaves in a wall of ice.

Serving ice creams and sorbets, parfaits and granitas in a bowl of ice invokes the ultimate chill factor. Added to that, it is a delightful way to preserve garlands of flowers, fruit, and foliage. With its solid wall of ice, up to about 1 inch thick, an ice bowl will keep its cool for about 2 hours—long enough for you to serve an elegant dessert and receive the delighted compliments of your guests. You can make small individual bowls, too. What could be prettier than a swirl of pastel pink rose-petal sorbet served in an ice bowl encasing a ring of miniature roses?

BOWLED OVER

You can easily make an ice bowl by using two freezer-proof mixing or serving bowls of different sizes. They should fit one inside the other, leaving a gap all round for the ice wall to be formed. Or you can buy an ice-bowl set. One has two bowls which clip together to make a bowl with a 2-pint capacity.

Building up the fruit or flower decoration, and freezing the bowl in stages, puts you in control of the design. Try to complete the operation all at once and the laws of physics will get the better of you. The flowers will float to the top and all semblance of a garland shape will be lost.

To make a bowl with a frosted look, you can use water straight from the tap. For one which is clearly transparent, use distilled water, or water which has been boiled and cooled.

To begin the decoration, pour about $1/2$ inch of water into the larger bowl and arrange a pattern of your chosen materials. You might like to make a ring of sliced strawberries or pansy flowers, for example. Place the bowl in the freezer, checking that it is standing level. When the water has frozen, pour on some more chilled water to cover the decoration and freeze it again.

Place the second bowl inside the first and, if it does not have clips, place a heavy weight in the center to prevent it from floating. Pour water between the two bowls and, using a wooden skewer to position them, arrange flowers or other materials in a ring around the circumference. Freeze the bowl again, and repeat the process to make one or two more garlands.

To unmold the ice bowl, wipe both inner and outer surfaces with a cloth wrung out in hot water and twist the two bowls to release the ice shape. Return it to the freezer until you are ready to present it.

Check that any flowers and leaves you use to decorate an ice bowl are edible. Besides earlier suggestions, you might like to add border pink, geranium petals, lavender, marigold, mint, nasturtium, orchid, rosemary, and sweet william.

Hoop of Delight

If you are serving a dessert or a selection of chilled fruits in a glass bowl, make it the center of attention by ringing it around with a hoop of flowers. Cool-looking peaches and cream colors, or a clash of reds, purples, and pinks, both schemes would look wonderful. Choose flowers that last well out of water—roses, carnations, spray carnations, and marigolds among them—and give them ample time to recover in water as soon as you bring them in. Measure the circumference of the bowl, cut a piece of wire long enough to allow for the join, or use a slender twig ring, and wire on separate flowers or sprays to make a continuous hoop. Spray the hoop with cool water and keep it out of the heat until it is needed. Fix it to the rim of the bowl with a few dabs of floral clay.

Above: For a cool-looking centerpiece, garland a glass bowl with a hoop of flowers, fill it with water and float pretty candles and rose petals in the center, or fill it with chilled summer fruits.

A MANTLE OF FLOWERS

Floral garlands know no bounds. In keeping with centuries of tradition, they can adorn our homes and embellish our attire, as two contrasting examples will show. One, a soft, petally circlet of flowers as bright as a summer's day, lifts a classic straw boater into the garden-party class. The other, composed of scarlet gerberas on a raffia tie, rivals the bold check curtains for style and impact.

You might be planning a *déjeuner sur l'herbe* with friends and family to while away the leisure hours on one of summer's golden days. You might be in the mood to trail your fingers dreamily in the water while someone expertly steers a boat through shady backwaters. Or you might be invited to a country wedding among an arbor of flowers. Whatever the occasion, a classic straw hat encircled with summer's prettiest flowers will be equal to it.

Above: The floral hatband is composed on a wire circle tightly bound with raffia. Then, if there is any show-through between the flowers, the ring will be scarcely discernible against the straw hat.

Right: For a prettily informal look, balance the floral shapes and colors around the band without aiming for perfect symmetry.

To make the floral hatband, measure around the crown of the hat, and cut and bind a length of flexible wire to fit it loosely, allowing a little extra length to avoid crushing the flowers. Bind the wire ring with raffia.

Gather a handful of flowers that have long-lasting credentials—pinks, cornflowers, freesias, and carnations among them—and the lightest-looking leaves you can find. Variegated pineapple mint, periwinkle, and lady's mantle are good choices.

Keep the flowers in water in a cool, shady place until the last possible moment. Then, when you are ready to compose the decoration, wipe the plant stems dry, and gather the flowers and leaves into mixed or all-of-a-kind posies.

Tie a length of raffia to the wire ring and bind on the first cluster of stems. Continue positioning and binding each bunch or individual flower to cover the stem ends of the one before, until the ring is covered.

Spray the decoration with cool water and keep it in a cool place for as long as you can. Attach the garland to the hat with a few dabs of floral clay or modeling clay, or with a couple of stitches.

ALL TIED UP

Floral curtain ties can do as much as any well-chosen flower arrangement to set the scene for a party. If the furnishing drapes are plain or just textured, then a "posy ring" style like the hatband would match the mood of high summer. Boldly-patterned curtains are best complemented by a stronger floral statement. Choose feature flowers such as carnations, zinnias, dahlias or gerberas to avoid a look of confusion and to create an impact.

The tie is simply made of a bundle of raffia strands tied around at intervals. After a long drink overnight in cool water, the gerberas are pinned to the raffia to make a continuous, edge-to-edge garland.

Left: Scarlet gerberas on a raffia tie make a bold decoration around checked curtain drapes. White flowers would look equally elegant.

Late Summer

The season of mellow fruitfulness, harvest, and Thanksgiving, late summer glows with opportunities to compose celebratory wreaths and garlands. Gather together fallen leaves and brilliant berries, golden fruits and vibrant vegetables, sun-bright flowers and sun-bleached seedheads, for designs with lasting appeal.

HARVEST THANKSGIVING

The colors of ripened corn and newly-plowed fields, of bright blue sky and the late summer sun, provide the inspiration for wreaths and garlands created to celebrate the season of Thanksgiving. These designs have a simplicity that has characterized such decorations since ancient times, when ears of wheat and bundles of corn were woven into the fabric of the festival as symbols of fertility on the land.

The combination of golden foliage and fruits, and brilliant blue flowers, is as natural as a day in the harvest fields is long. Take these colors as your theme and you can express it in a variety of ways, setting the scene for a harvest supper or a Thanksgiving get-together outdoors.

Create areas of interest beyond the buffet or serving table so that the entire party arena becomes a stage for the festivities. String harvest garlands from the branches of a tree, or high above a gateway or other entrance, where they will greet guests as they approach.

You can thread a "necklace" of fallen leaves in shades of red to russet, or bind branches of golden leaves together to form a string. Or, closer to the harvest theme, create a garland of dried sweet corn (Indian corn) cobs, including, if you can, some decorative varieties for their wide color range. Pull up

Above: Silhouetted against the sky, a garland of dried corncobs is as casual as it is appropriate. To set the party scene indoors, string the garland over a door or suspend it above a buffet table.

Right: The golden and blue table ring is composed of elements which contrast not only in color, but also in form and style. Bundles of miniature corn and wheat stalks alternate around the circle with quinces and spray carnations.

the parchment-dried leaves high above the seedheads, like birds on the wing, and bind each one to the rope core with flexible wire.

Miniature sweet corn cobs, readily available in supermarkets, play a part in harvest decorations on a smaller scale. Gather three or four cobs into a bundle, tie them together with raffia or string, and partner them with fruit and flowers to capture the mood of the season. The table wreath featured was composed on a wet foam ring, with bundles of corn and longer, thinner bunches of wheat stalks, similarly tied and wired onto false stems. Yellowing maple leaves and spray carnations vie with golden quince, also wired for color-brightness, and are contrasted with mauvy-blue iris flowers. A fan of wheat ears provides both symbolism and continuity, carrying on harvest traditions whose origins are lost in time.

The same color elements can be interpreted in a different way, in a still-life group set out under the shade of an overhanging tree. Slender branches of yellow-brown beech leaves are bound onto a thin twig wreath form and placed as if they belong there, on a pile of logs. Bowls of golden and green squash, including the pumpkin-like munchkins, and jugs of flowers complete a delightfully informal focus of interest.

Left: A ring of gold, a twig wreath bound with dried-on-the-hedge beech leaves, is grouped with harvest fruits and garden flowers in a simple interpretation of the harvest theme.

PICTURE FRAMED

Take a favorite pen-and-ink sketch or print, a watercolor or an etching, take any picture you like, put it in a complementary frame and compose a fulsome swag of fruits and foliage around it. The arrangement becomes a secondary work of art, while the picture remains the focus of attention.

Gilded pineapple tops, cones and fallen leaves, false fruits and berries, together create an illusion of opulence around an early 19th-century print of a young milkmaid.

The print is framed in a simple surround of bleached Australian driftwood, its soft greeny-gray tones a perfect foil for the subtle coloring of the farmyard scene. The natural wood also provides a strong contrast to the richness of the decorative materials, from the.berry bright to the inky black.

Vertical swags can fulfill a variety of decorative functions in a room. A single swag can add interest when it is hung between two wall timbers, in a narrow alcove or between two pieces of furniture. A pair of matching swags composed around companion pictures can emphasize strong architectural features such as a fireplace, door or archway, or add charm and sentiment when they are displayed on each side of the bed.

Above: A heavy raffia plait, a framed 19th-century print, "Milk O!," and a few of the design elements show the contrasting shapes and textures that will comprise the swag.

Left: The design builds up. Above the print, a profusion of apricot-colored fruits and wine-red berries, pine cones, and dried leaves is arranged layer on layer, with each element firmly wired into the plait and the stems of each succeeding element covering those of the ones before.

The swag in the photograph was composed on a thick raffia plait of the type you can make or buy. This one, with its large braided loop, provides a visual balance to the apparent weight of the materials used. Some of these, the fallen foliage and dried bay leaves, the larch cones and pine cones, are *objets trouves* to be gathered on a country walk. Others, the bunches of frosted fruits and clusters of glowing berries, are widely available from florists. The gilded pineapple tops, a finishing touch of true opulence, provide a surprise note of glamor.

The build-up to the decoration begins by firmly attaching the picture to the plait. Use pliable roll wire for this, taking it through the loops on the back of the frame and around the raffia.

Use medium-gauge floral wires (stub wires) to mount each group of decorative items. Starting at the top, just below the loop, arrange the wired materials so that they contrast well in both color and form. Push the false wire stems firmly among the raffia strands and build up the design layer by layer. Make sure that some elements, dried leaves or small berry clusters, overlap the picture frame to break up the horizonal lines. Build up the other end of the swag in a similar way, beginning close to the base and working towards the center.

Right: *The use of a large braided loop provides balance to the apparent weight of the decorative natural materials.*

RINGING TONES

Above: A basket of stones, treasure trove from an excursion to the beach, is a rich source of materials for decorative rings and garlands.

Left: A necklace made of threaded stones looks especially good against backgrounds of plain, muted colors. These stones were selected for their color tones, from mussel-shell gray to orangy-brown.

Turn a stroll along the beach into a treasure hunt for stones with millions-of-years-old holes, then thread them to make a designer necklace to decorate your home. Collect other stones for their unusual shapes and color configurations, and you can arrange them to garland a pretty glass plate or serving dish to set the style for a seafood supper or special picnic.

Gather a handful of stones from any beach and you are handling the rocks of ages. Depending on where you live or take your vacation, the stones you turn over in your palms will give you a fascinating insight into the pre-history of the place. They might be pieces of igneous rock, formed eons ago in intense heat when molten materials solidified; sedimentary rocks formed of layer upon layer of sediment laid down on the seabed; or metamorphic rocks, which over time have absorbed new materials and recrystallized into a different form.

It might be the form and color of the stones you collect that inspires you to display them around the home in ingenious ways. Collecting stones with natural holes is a treasure hunt of finely tuned proportions, though those in the photographs were found on a beach in northern France in a couple of hours. Boring holes with a special masonry drill is likely to take rather longer.

To form heavy stones into a wreath that will hold its circular shape, thread them on heavy-gauge, pliable wire and bind the overlapping ends with narrow floral adhesive tape. If you use wire for the binding, the ends tend to spring apart.

To make a necklace loop, which need not hold a rigid shape, use any strong, natural material that empathizes with the stones. Leather thonging, rough string or fine cord all look good, the ends being tied into a simple knot or loop. Hang the stone necklace on a wall hook, or display it on a windowsill or window seat where, especially in the winter, the natural light will flatter the character of the stones.

Select smaller, flatter stones to ring around or form a circle under a glass plate, to bring a hint of the seashore to a seafood meal or a beachside picnic. A small glass underplate gives form to the stone circle, and remains in place when the dinner plates are removed.

Right: An opaque glass dinner plate gives a misty look to the garland of flat stones arranged around a glass underplate. A single stone with a natural hole is threaded on leather for a companion napkin ring.

TROPICAL ILLUSION

F ragrant herbs and cottage garden flowers, succulent rosehips and Singapore orchids, encircle a contrasting central feature, a contorted willow stem held in a dish of marble chippings. It's a decoration that could be all things to all occasions. It is graceful and stylish enough to take center-stage on a formal dinner table, bold and cheeky enough to be the decorative focus of attention when guests gather around the barbecue or the pool.

As the brilliant blooms around the ring seem to shimmer in the heat, there is the cooling effect of a dish of clear water in the center. A metal pinholder keeps the contorted willow stem firmly in place, and is concealed beneath a handful of marble chippings. A single stem of magenta Singapore orchid entwined around the central stem creates a horticultural illusion.

The flowers arranged in the wet foam ring are as bright as can be, proof that floral colors have not reached saturation point, however late in the season. The simple daisy shapes of pot marigolds are color coordinated with trumpet-shaped nasturtiums in orange and gold. Somewhere along the rainbow between clear red and true mauve, the magenta orchid flowers contribute an element of luxury among the garden-gathered materials.

As with the dish of cool, clear water, so with the foliage. The sprays of variegated scented geranium and pineapple mint, the leaves more cream than green, serve to emphasize the vibrance of the colors around them.

Right: With its brilliant color contrasts and eye-catching central feature, this is a decoration that can set either a formal or a relaxed tone.

CIRCLES OF LIGHT

Above: A slender circle of intertwined twigs is a suitable base for a willowy wreath, since it will allow the maximum light penetration.

Right: Display the wreath where the natural or artificial light can shine through the leaves, to emphasize their fragile-seeming translucence.

Traveler's joy, old man's beard, *Clematis vitalba*, call it what you will, this and other similar twisting and twirling hedgerow plants are irresistible garland material. Carefully unwind a few trailing stems from neighboring shrubs and trees, and wind them around a wreath base or a basket. The last rays of the summer sun will recreate the effect of circles of light.

When the mood is relaxed and carefree, when you are planning an outdoor gathering, or you just feel like celebrating the last days of summer, turn to the waysides and hedgerows for design inspiration.

Choosing a single plant species to wind into wreath and garland forms is a way of creating decorations of delightful simplicity. You might choose yellowing leaves of hop vine or light-colored ivy foliage, the red-going-on-purple leaves of blackberry bramble, or wild rose and juicy-berry hips.

Our choice was *Clematis vitalba*, which is affectionately known by a variety of country names in the regions where it rambles profusely in late summer. It is an ideal "garland" plant. With its pale yellowy-green and translucent leaves, it seems to attract every shaft of the setting sun, and then to glow, softly, through the evening's shadows. Gather leafy

trails when the fruits are ripe and, with their long, silvery awns, they look like cotton tufts or clusters of shimmering snowflakes. It is this tactile, fluffy characteristic that gives the plant its popular name, old man's beard.

For a simple garland to hang in the window, from a branch of a tree or as a wall or door decoration, you can wind several long stems into a circle and bind the ends where they overlap. Or, for a more substantial form, you can bind them with silver floral wire or green twine to a slender twig ring.

If your chosen stem lengths are not amply covered with a profusion of fluffy fruits, cut a few short stems from others and tuck them into the wreath circle to recreate the hedge-row look.

The simplicity of a single plant garland can be put to stunning effect in a different way, in a display of mouth-watering fruits or exotic flowers. Wind the stems around a garden table, or a wicker tray fixed to a bundle of twigs, and the unpretentious garland will add immeasurably to the overall effect.

Left: Contrast a collection of brilliantly-colored fruits, from scarlet tamarillos to golden kumquats, with a simple hedgerow garland for a memorable effect.

FRUITFUL ENDEAVORS

Above: Thickly-sliced rosy apples with their star-shaped centers, orange slices, and whole oranges are ready for oven drying.

Right: Whole dried oranges, their skins burnt umber colored and leathery, are contrasted with sprays of dried berries and bay leaves in a wreath that could take its place in a kitchen or sitting room.

Gather a bountiful harvest of rosy apples or buy a bag of zingy citrus fruits, dry them, and compose them into garlands and wreaths of lasting decorative value. These homey designs are inspired by the delightful simplicity of those traditional to the American Shaker community.

Drying whole or sliced fruits has for centuries been practiced as a practical and efficient way of preserving them. In the years when the harvest was good and the apple baskets quickly filled, it was a time of nonstop activity in the kitchen as the fruits were sliced, spread in a single layer on muslin-covered trays, and put out to dry in the sun.

This method of drying not only apples, but also pears and citrus fruits, is still as practicable today. A handful of parchment-colored, rosy-skinned dried apple rings has definite "bite" appeal, and eye-appeal, too. Even as they dry, a line of apple rings makes a decorative feature strung from side to side of a dry, airy kitchen. If you do decide to dry fruit in this way, on strings instead of trays, knot the string between each slice so that warm air can circulate between them and gradually draw the moisture from the whole surface of the fruit.

Another way is to slice the fruits, apples or pears, oranges, lemons, and limes. Then spread the slices in a single layer on a

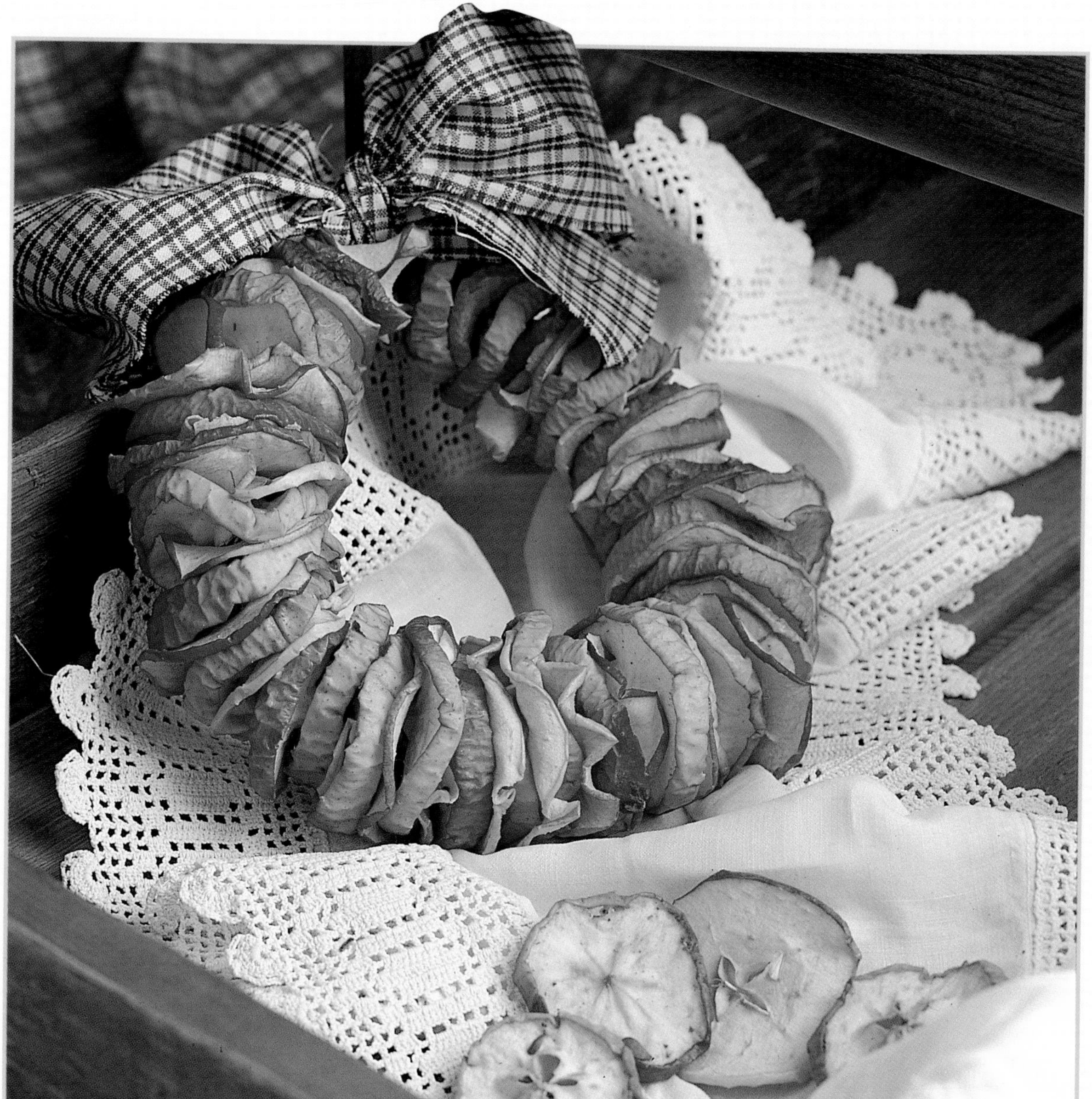

Left: Red-skinned apple slices are threaded onto thick, pliable wire and decorated with a simple cotton gingham bow for a traditional kitchen decoration.

Above: Dried orange rings and bay leaves alternate to make a colorful and aromatic garland to decorate a chair back, a kitchen wall or door. Complete the circle by joining the two ends of the wire and you have a pretty kitchen wreath.

wire cake rack and dry them in the oven at the lowest setting for six to eight hours, turning them over if possible. Not all varieties of apples and pears discolor quickly once they are cut, but some do. To preserve their natural color, drop the slices straight away into a bowl of acidulated water (3 tbsp citric acid and the juice of 1 lemon to each 1/2 pint of water) and leave them for five minutes. Drain the slices and dry them on paper towels.

Drying whole oranges or limes extends the shape of designs to come. To do this, make six or eight slits vertically through to the center of the fruit, without cutting right through it, and dry it in a low-temperature oven for eight to ten hours, turning it once if possible.

MAKING THE DECORATIONS

Once they are thoroughly dry, and cooled, sliced fruits can be threaded into rings and garlands, and whole ones glued or wired to wreath bases. In keeping with the spirit of such decorations, combine the fruits with dried bay leaves and spices. Bundles of cinnamon sticks tied with raffia, and star anise pods glued to the center of apple or orange rings, both add not only style but also the lingering scents of a busy kitchen.

HALLOWEEN HAPPENINGS

Above: Small candles cast a warm glow over the friendly face of the pumpkin jack-o'-lantern. The smiling character is surrounded by a garland of fallen maple leaves dried in the sun until they curl at the edges.

Right: A decorative interpretation of the traditional apple-bobbing tub, an old iron barbecue is fitted with a glass bowl and garlanded with threaded mulberry leaves.

In the witching hours before the dawn of All Saint's Day on November 1st, the evening belongs to ghoullies and ghosties and long-legged beasties; and also to fun and frolics, jollity and high jinks. Set the scene for a Halloween party with garlands of colorful fallen leaves, an apple-bobbing tub, and a traditional jack-o'-lantern, and your guests will be in high spirits.

At this time of year, gardens and country lanes are carpeted with fallen leaves in shades from sunshine gold to warm chestnut brown, some as fresh as the moment they fluttered to the ground, and others sun-dried and curling attractively at the edges. Gather them all to give your party setting a free and easy look.

Color and shape will contribute immeasurably to your decorations, so select leaves that will rival the glowing pumpkins for intensity of light. The foliage of Norway maple (*Acer platanoides*), tulip tree (*Liriodendron tulipifera*), Sweet gum (*Liquidamber styraciflua*), and yellow buckeye (*Aesculus flava*) are brilliant examples that will catch every shaft of the setting sun and every flicker of candlelight.

Size up the party area in advance, and plan where you can stage the decorations to maximum effect. Garlands of threaded leaves look stunning against a dark wall or fence, or simply

Left: An old weatherboarded barn is decked out for the occasion with a garland of threaded leaves strung from side to side of every window and door.

Above: Butternut and golden nugget squash, acorn squash, and pumpkins, they all have hidden personalities waiting to be revealed as Halloween lanterns.

strung from branch to branch of a barren tree and outlined against the night sky.

Choose fresh, supple leaves for a garland. The flat shapes are more clearly defined and more dramatic, and the soft sappy stems are easier to thread. Using a darning needle and black or colorless thread, string as many leaves as it takes to outline a window, door or porch, or highlight a barn or carport.

Collect and thread more leaves to surround the apple-bobbing tub. This traditional Halloween feature can be for decoration only or, if your guests take kindly to the joyful indignity of full-face immersion, it can become all part of the fun. If the game is for real, choose apples which are small enough for participants to snatch them in one bite.

Crisp and crackly dried leaves make a shapely garland around each jack-o'-lantern. To make this characteristic decoration, you can choose any type of squash. Cut a thin slice from the top and, with a large spoon, scoop out the seeds and loose fibers. Draw a face with a marker pen—happy and smiling or fierce and menacing, as you please—and cut out the features with a small, sharp knife. Insert nightlights or votive candles in the lantern, set the lid at a jaunty angle, so that smoke can escape, and let a mood of high spirits take over.

OF CABBAGES AND RINGS

The last flowers of summer and the market stall's most colorful vegetables come together as happily as (with apologies to Lewis Carroll) "cabbages and rings." Go for a color theme, as bold as you dare, then go for the design components that will most dramatically carry it through, from the rosiest spindle fruits bound around a twig wreath to the shiniest eggplants highlighting a wet foam ring.

If you have access to a profusion of wild fruits or berries, hips or haws, the temptation is to bind them onto a large wreath frame and hang it, resplendent, as a long-lasting hall decoration. And why not? It's the brightest, zingiest design around at Thanksgiving and harvest-time, a splash of brilliance when all around might be sun-bleached gold and parched-earth brown.

A delightful interpretation of this idea is a diminutive version of it, a half-covered twig ring displayed as an accessory to a country-style composition of flowers and vegetables. The woody ring is decorated half-way around with clusters of spindle fruits (*Euonymus europaeus*), the bright pink seeds bursting out from even brighter orange casings.

Long stems of the fruiting shrub define the extremities of the arrangement, composed in a hand-thrown earthenware pot. Bright green foliage provides

Right: An accessory after the fact, a small twig ring is part-covered with sprays of spindle fruits – you could use rosehip or rowan berries – and placed as an extension to the informal arrangement of flowers and vegetables.

color and textural contrasts, and the design is filled in with small purple eggplants (pierced by satay sticks), hollyhocks, and a few of the last blush-pink roses of summer. Small heads of crinkly-leaved ornamental cabbage (a bright shade of purple, too) complete the informal group.

TABLE DECORATIONS

With a marked shift of emphasis, the other ring is all set to be the center of attraction at a dinner party or on a buffet table. Brilliant green chilies, speared on wooden toothpicks, are added to the component list, and chosen not only for their contrasting color, but also for their high-gloss factor.

With design ingredients like these, your guests' attention is guaranteed. Talk-up your table setting still further by creating a flower and vegetable posy to decorate the table napkin at each place. Bind together a few sprays of berries or fruits, a single rose and a cluster of ornamental cabbage leaves, and tuck them under a gossamer ribbon bow. It's called flattery!

Left: Purple, pink, and bright green makes an alluring composition for a table center. The wet foam ring is first arranged with small eggplants and chilies pierced on wooden sticks and positioned this way and that, then filled with clematis foliage and spindle sprays, ornamental cabbage leaves and two-tone pink flowers.

WINTER

As daylight gives way to lamplight and the flicker of candle flames, switch on to decorative materials that reflect the festive spirit. Glossy evergreens, metallic papers, zingy fruits, false berries, burnished metals, and shiny ribbons all contribute to the season's brightest decorations, from traditional welcome wreaths to dramatic table presentations.

LIVING LEGENDS

Hoops and rings, wreaths, and circlets of ivy are the most traditional of all Christmas decorations. First the pagans and then the early Christians associated both holly and ivy with good luck and with rebirth, a sign that spring was not far away. They vested them with magical powers, too, being unable to explain in any other way the evergreen plants' ability to retain their leaves when trees about them were bare. Add to centuries of tradition the fact that both plants when cut last for at least the twelve days of Christmas, and you have the ideal decorative materials.

As you start searching the countryside to decorate your home, you will soon realize that ivy is a plant of immense variety or, strictly speaking, of numerous varieties. Whilst the instantly recognisable common ivy (*Hedera helix*), with its familiar, near-triangular leaf shape, represents for most of us the "true" ivy, there are around 400 other varieties to consider as the raw materials for your decorations.

Some have their roots firmly planted in the past. Not long after the birth of Christ, Pliny the Elder chronicled the differing characteristics of the ivy, noting that there was a grass-green variety "which is the commonest, a second kind with a white leaf and a third with a variegated leaf." He also drew attention to the ivy berry as a variable decorative feature by noting "one kind with black seed and another a seed the color of saffron, the latter is

Right: A hoop of ivy above an earthenware flowerpot could be shaped from a living plant. This one, with the look of living topiary, is formed of long ivy trails cut, given a long drink in water, then bound to a twig ring.

used by poets for their wreaths." Even now the latter variety, Poet's Ivy (*Hedera helix var. poetica*), is valued for the striking color contrast between its golden berries and deep green foliage.

The potential of ivy as a topiary plant to be shaped in representational and whimsical ways has long been acknowledged. A collection of such shapes in a garden in the United States, in Pennsylvania, even includes life-size carousel animals.

If there is no time to fashion complicated forms and characters from the living plant, a hoop of ivy can be displayed as a false topiary, standing on end and fixed to dry floral foam in a flowerpot. A similar wreath, in keeping with long tradition, makes a verdant wall decoration embellished for the occasion with gilded fruits and trailing ribbons.

Right: A hint of gold in the background and the adornments adds sparkle to a traditional hoop of common ivy. The foliage ring is decorated with gold-sprayed pomegranates pierced with floral wires.

FRUIT FOR THOUGHT

Above: A foam ring covered with bay leaves, and first decorated with wayward bunches of slender twigs, becomes gradually more colorful as the fruits are speared on sticks or threaded on non-corrosive wires.

Right: Slices of glistening star fruit and individual orchid flowers provide the finishing touches in a decorative fresh fruit ring that would make an exotic centerpiece for a buffet table.

Think of fruit as components for wreaths and garlands and the imagination wanders from the simple to the extravagant, the irresistible to the fantastic. Between them, the designs on these pages might merit all these descriptions and, so different in both concept and appearance, demonstrate the versatility of fruit in the round. One thing they do have in common—both decorations are certain conversation pieces.

Fresh pineapple and lychees, pomegranates and Chinese gooseberries, or false apples and pears, peaches and plums— arranged in a circle and positioned in the center of the table, either decoration is a hard visual act to follow, no matter how delicious the food.

Fruit has been associated with entertaining and feasting since Roman times, when it was piled high to set the scene for banquets of legendary proportions. Nowadays, it does not necessarily come easily to cast financial caution to the winds and splash out on a basketful of fresh fruits to decorate a table, however significant the occasion. But if the event is short-lived, such as a dinner party or a single-day celebration, you and your guests can appreciate the visual delights of the fruits at the time, before they are reclaimed as ingredients.

For this reason, the fresh fruit ring was composed using only noncorrosive fixing materials. After the foam ring was

covered with fresh bay leaves (pinned in place with wire staples), the lychees and kumquats were speared on wooden cocktail sticks. The pomegranates and pineapple were threaded on a double thickness of heavy-gauge, plastic-covered wire which was then wrapped tightly around the foam ring. Cape gooseberries (*physalis*) are no problem. Wires can be wrapped around the top of the seed and beneath the papery covering. Slices of star fruit and limes are easily speared on wooden sticks. They could be better preserved for eating later by being covered with a disc of plastic wrap.

It's All an Illusion

The question of edibility does not arise with the fruits in the wire-covered ring. That decoration is all about mixing and matching the brightest and best of the fruits, regardless of the season. The most realistic ones might be molded from plastic or papier-mâché, and many defy credibility. Be prepared for guests to prod the ring surreptitiously to check out the fruits' credentials.

The ring is made of a narrow strip of wire mesh netting wrapped around the fruits and bent round to form a circle. Wire ends must be tucked in methodically so that they do not scratch the table, and joined ends of the circle lashed together with silver wire. True or false, fruits in the round make eye-catching decorations.

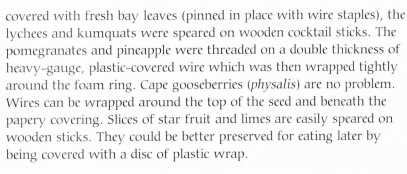

Left: A table ring with the longest decorative life of all. The fruits enclosed in the wire hoop are all molded look-alikes in plastic or papier-mâché.

SHAKER STYLE

Above: The elements of a Shaker-style decoration—a heart shaped from slender twigs, bunches of herbs, and a copper-heart tree ornament.

Right: *Side by side on a cottage wall, two Shaker heart shapes are minimally decorated with bunches of santolina and rosemary, with dried sweet corn and quilted cotton ornaments. Beeswax candles in pinewood trugs reinforce the Shaker theme.*

Heart shapes fashioned from twigs and sparsely decorated with cotton ornaments and fragrant herbs have widespread appeal, reaching far beyond the Shaker community in the United States where they became traditional. There is a long tradition, too, for creating decorative wreaths from fabric scraps, exemplifying the "waste not, want not" dictum in a variety of attractive ways.

Long before the term minimalist was used to describe a decorative style, the Shakers, who formed large communal societies throughout the northeastern States of America, well understood the value of restraint in furnishing design. Many of their clothes, homespun and colored with home-grown dye plants, were characterized by the use of checks, from bold red and black woven chequerboard squares to more subtle gingham patterns of, variously, red, green, blue or black blended with parchment-cream fibers.

These fabrics seem as fresh today as they did when the utopian communities were founded in the 19th century, from Maine in the north down to Kentucky. Cut out heart shapes, stars, fish, mittens, boottees, animals or simple rag doll designs from checked cotton and your decorations will follow the Shaker pattern. (To give white-checked gingham cottons the softer, more homely look of Shaker materials, dye them in a weak solution of tea.)

Circular and heart-shaped wreaths, which might be hidden beneath a generous covering of evergreens or herbs, can be decorative features in their own right. Bind bunches of long-lasting aromatic leaves such as santolina or sage, bay, rosemary or lavender at intervals around the wreath form, add dried miniature corn cobs, pieces cut from larger cobs, or bundles of small beeswax candles tied on with raffia, and then cotton decorations as you will. Angels, snowmen, and St. Nicholas and the long checked cotton stockings he comes to fill might restrict the wallhangings to the Christmas season, while other shapes—from cats and scarecrows to quilted drawstring bags—have a more lasting quality.

RAG-RUG WREATH

Not all the items made from wool and cotton scraps were utilitarian in the way that quilts and rugs were. Other make-over designs were created, no expense needed, from used garments given a new and decorative lease of life. The woollen wreath shown on these pages is an example of such a design, made from 3-inch squares of red, green, and gray tartan wool threaded onto heavy-gauge, flexible wire.

The style element is assured by using materials in toning or complementary colors or, as in this case, making a wreath from a single discarded garment. It is important to use enough squares so that, when the threaded length is wrapped around into a circle, there is a clearly visible hole in the center. Otherwise, it will appear as an indefinable mass.

Left: A rag-rug wreath made from woollen squares is styled to complement a collection of red enamelware. To the left, a smaller wreath, made from scraps of chamois leather, could serve a useful as well as a decorative purpose.

HAPPY FAMILIES

Joining hands and forming a garland over a fireplace or from branch to branch of the Christmas tree—gingerbread people have been doing just that for generations. The characters in this garland have a different origin. They are made from thick apple sauce and powdered cinnamon, mixed to a paste and dried out over six or seven days. It's a recipe for successful garlands to delight the children and encourage their eager participation.

The tradition of enjoying spiced cookies cut out to resemble people, animals, and houses is thought to have originated in Germany, where guilds of gingerbread artisans were formed as long ago as the 14th century. It was not until the 18th century, when the Grimms' fairy tale of Hansel and Gretel described a house "made of bread, with a roof of cake and windows of barley," that the decorations became popular with all levels of society.

Describing homes on both sides of the Atlantic, observers would now note that from Thanksgiving to Christmas cardboard wreaths covered with iced gingerbread figures decorate children's party tables and bedroom doors; garlands of spiced cookies alternating with bay leaves and cinnamon sticks are hung as necklaces over doors and windows, fireplaces and furniture; and rings of cut-out human shapes might be arranged, like maypole dancers, around deep dessert dishes or even flowerpots.

Right: Strung from side to side of a fireplace beam, the garland makes an amusing decoration for a child's room. The pine branches add another seasonal dimension, and the tartan bow a brightly-colored focal point.

The figures in our fireplace garland, just as spicy as any gingerbread men, have the advantage that they will not so readily become soft and can be kept satisfactorily (in an airtight container) from year to year. Added to that, they do not need baking, and so they are safer and easier for young children to make.

SPICED APPLE SAUCE FIGURES

1 lb sweetened apple sauce, canned or fresh
about 4 oz wholewheat flour
about 4 oz ground cinnamon

Drain the apple sauce overnight in a sieve over a bowl.

Gradually beat in the flour and ground cinnamon alternately, until the mixture forms a stiff, dry dough.

Divide the dough into four equal parts, and roll it out between sheets of parchment paper to a thickness of 1/4 inch. Cut out gingerbread men shapes and prick holes with a skewer through their hands. Gather the trimmings into a ball and roll out the dough to make more.

Transfer the figures to a wire cake rack and leave in a warm, dry place such as an airing cupboard. Turn the shapes once a day for six or seven days, until they are dry and hard.

Brush the figures with a little ground cinnamon to give them a more toasty appearance.

Thread the figures alone or with other decorative components to make a garland.

Above: Cinnamon-brown apple sauce dough is rolled out between sheets of parchment paper and cut out in gingerbread men shapes.

Right: Clusters of dried bay leaves and bundles of cinnamon sticks tied with shiny ribbons are threaded with cinnamon and apple sauce figures to form a jolly garland.

BIRDSEED WREATHS

D on't forget the small garden birds in wintertime. They might be content with a few crumbs or a bowl of birdseed, but wreaths and garlands strung on bare tree branches are more aesthetically pleasing for the human population to see. The feeders are no trouble to make, and look all the more attractive for the addition of simple ribbon bows.

Necklaces of peanuts threaded on twine beckon not only to the birds but also to the neighborhood squirrels, and may soon be spirited away little by little for safekeeping in underground storehouses. Keeping watch to see which species claims the tasty prize can be a fascinating and leisurely pastime.

More focused facilities are provided for small birds by the birdseed wreaths, as they are as easy to land on and swing on as any perch can be. The wreath bases can be made of bound or closely interwoven twigs, straw, supple stems like grass and bryony, or any other type you care to consign for use and re-use by garden visitors. Follow the instructions in the "recipe," and leave the wreath to set in the refrigerator overnight before hanging it on strings or ribbons. If you have a steady stream of garden birds, it is a nice idea to have two alternating wreaths, with one setting in the fridge while the other is hung out for the hungry hordes.

Left: Garlands of threaded peanuts to nurture the squirrels and birdseed wreaths to feed the small birds—a small apple tree becomes a focal point of interest in the garden.

Top: Hold each wreath base with tongs and dip into the suet mixture. Use a spoon to coat the inside of the ring and crevices.

Above: Dip the suet-coated ring in birdseed and pat it into the surface to cover it on all sides. Mixture for small birds contains seeds in a wide variety of colors.

Right: Set in a ring mold and in patty pans, these birdseed treats can be served in style, on a table or plank crossing.

If you prefer to give birds their alfresco meal from a table or other horizontal surface, make them a birdseed mold in a ring form pan and decorate that, too, with ribbon bows. After all, who wants to look out from the kitchen window on an unadorned ring mold made from melted suet and birdseed? The seed "cakes" are made from a similar mixture, poured into patty pans and set in the refrigerator overnight.

TO MAKE THE BIRD WREATHS

3 6-in wreath bases • 1 lb suet, grated
4 oz peanut butter • 4 oz fine semolina
about 12 oz birdseed for small birds
ribbon, for hanging

Melt the suet in a large, shallow pan over low heat, and stir in the peanut butter and semolina. Spread the birdseed in a shallow dish.

Turn off the heat and, holding each wreath with tongs, dip it first into the fat mixture, spooning it over the inside so that the whole surface is coated.

Still holding the wreath with tongs, dip it into the birdseed, pressing the mixture onto the surface with the back of a spoon.

Refrigerate the wreaths overnight before hanging on ribbons.

GREEN, GOLD, & GLORIOUS

Above: Beeswax candles in dark holly green are a perfect match for the verdigris candlestick with its long ribbon-trail of juniper and miniature parcels.

Right: Two cherubic verdigris musicians are attached with colorless thread to an oval wreath composed of ivy and juniper leaves. The decoration would make an unusual welcome wreath for the front door.

An oval-shaped wall wreath of mixed evergreens adorned with verdigris cherubim; a matching candlestick garlanded with a ribbon of trailing greenery and tiny gold-wrapped parcels; a made-to-match napkin trimming, and a gilded willow wreath decorated with a cluster of miniature parcels and a cherubic head—decorations that are green and gold make a glorious contribution to your home at Christmas.

Evergreen wreaths may be composed of a single plant species or a medley of two or more types, chosen for their contrasting leaf shapes, colors, and textures. Combine, as we have done, ivy foliage with feathery blue-gray sprays of juniper and cypress in a wreath that will alternately catch and hold, catch and reflect the light. Blend variegated holly or the equally bright yellow-green foliage of the elaeagnus leaf sprays with single-tone foliage, such as bay or eucalyptus, in a decoration that will benefit from the contrast of color highlights and more muted patches. Or compose a wreath of laurel leaves and overlay them at intervals with clusters of variegated ivy or lime-green cypress.

The oval wreath featured, so full of interest because of the complementary characteristics of the foliage, needs little adornment. A gold thread decoration at the top, reminiscent of a fleur-de-lis, is balanced by a pair of verdigris cherubim, each one playing a heavenly musical instrument.

BRAND IMAGE

If the wreath is to be displayed in the dining room or over a buffet table, it is a good idea to echo the theme in the table decorations, to give the area a coordinated and unified look. The twisted braid decoration is repeated in the form of a napkin ring at each place setting, and the verdigris and evergreen

theme carried out in the choice of candlesticks. A trail of slender juniper stems bound onto flexible wire and embellished with tiny pretend gift parcels says so much more than the undecorated candleholders might.

Any tall candlesticks can be decorated in a similar way, with trails of small-leaved foliage—it might be ivy or berberis, rosemary or yew—contrasted with clusters of berries, dried flowers or long-lasting fresh flowers, such as spray carnations and Christmas roses.

Above: A twist of gold braid wrapped around the base of the loops and pinned behind the napkin makes a flamboyant place setting decoration.

Left: It's gold and more gold in a paint-sprayed willow ring decorated with tiny parcels and a cherub's head. A delightful idea to hang over a bedpost or above a bed.

PARCEL WREATH

To complement decorations verdant with evergreen foliage, or to hang on the Christmas tree, compose an all-gold wreath which itself has contrasting textures. Paint or spray a willow wreath with matt gold and attach a cluster of decorative items to cover it halfway round. Go for glitter, and choose small gold baubles or gold "picks" already wired and looking like bunches of gilded grapes. Spray small fruits, such as lychees or a handful of mixed nuts, with gloss or matt gold paint or, as we have done, wrap a collection of mini parcels in gold crepe paper and tie them around with shiny thread. Stock-cube and similar boxes are just the right size for wrapping; or you could build up parcels of sugar cubes arranged to create a variety of shapes.

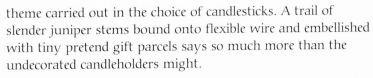

WINTER WONDERLAND

———————◆○◆———————

Hedgerows of crisscrossing twigs heavy with snow, or crackling with hoarfrost, and barren branches starkly outlined against a misty sky—these are the images of winter, a far cry from lush and glossy evergreens, captured in these minimalist wreaths. Hang them on plain, contrasting walls or doors to emphasize their striking silhouettes.

For thousands of years people have decked their homes in winter with a glorious profusion of greenery, appreciated for its glossy brightness and, in earlier times, marveled at for its year-round continuity. But there is beauty in the barrenness of bare deciduous branches, too, in their contortions and confusions, their twisty, twirly outlines, and their dramatic silhouettes. This colder-seeming and more graphic aspect of the countryside in winter is effectively recreated in these simple wall decorations. You can leave them starkly unadorned or, as we have done, embellish them with other seasonal images, pine cones, scarlet berries, and shimmering pine-tree-green bows.

To Make the Twig Wreath

The success of this decoration, composed of a crisscross of slender twigs, begins right there on the ground, with the selection of materials. Choose those with the most wayward habits, the greatest number of forks and off-shoots, and altogether the most untidy appearance.

Right: For the most dramatic effect, hang a bare-twig wreath against a plain white wall, or in a window where it will be silhouetted against a gray, wintry sky.

Bend a length of split cane or willow into a circle with a diameter of about 12 inches and bind the ends together, or use a ready-made wreath form, the thinnest you can find. Spread out the twigs in a single layer and ease them out to a roughly circular shape. Place the ring in the center and add more twigs if the pile looks too sparse.

Thread a carpet needle or candle-making wicking needle with thin string or twine, and bind the twigs to the ring, taking the "stitches" over and around all the layers. Cut a paper circle as a guide, place it over the twigs and cut all around the edge to make a roughly circular shape, though a few straggly twig ends are all part of the decoration's natural charm.

To decorate the center of the wreath, bind on lengths of false berry stems and wired pine cones and, unless the wreath will be exposed to unfavorable elements, add a bright ribbon bow.

A "Snow-Covered" Wreath

To highlight an inky-black wall or door, make a wreath that is a negative image of the natural twig one. Spray it with one of the imitation snow preparations, and decorate it with cones and berries or a simple ribbon in the shape of a bow.

Right: Looking even more delicate with its snowy white coating, this wreath makes an unusual welcome wreath, or a striking indoor decoration.

ACKNOWLEDGMENTS

The publishers would like to thank the following companies in the
United Kingdom for supplying materials:

glue gun by **Bostik**; Chinese baskets, key rack, patchwork throw,
pottery, tumblers, and vase from **Nice Irma's**, 0171-580-6921;
tableware by **Royal Doulton** and **Minton**; most of the ribbons used by
Offray (for stockists, telephone 01784-247281); plastic-cage garland core
by **Simply Garlands**, 01296-661425; and enamel bowl and tin lanterns
from **The Kasbah**, 0171-379-5230.